GETTING IN THE GAME

GETTING IN THE GAME

A Parent's Guide to Raising an Athlete

THOMAS LOTT

with THOMAS LOTT III

ISBN: 1517086493
ISBN 13: 9781517086497

CONTENTS

FOREWORD

RAISING A CHILD, while being a rewarding and life-changing experience, presents parents with a myriad of challenges. The bookshelves are overflowing with parental-guidance manuals filled with instructions on how to overcome many common obstacles on this long journey. However, few books are available that provide wise and experienced advice on how to successfully combine the fundamentals of child rearing with the complexities of concurrently introducing a young boy or girl to the world of competitive sports.

Within the pages of *Getting in the Game: A Parent's Guide to Raising an Athlete*, Thomas Lott draws upon his forty-five years of experience as a high school, college, and professional football player and coach to outline not only how to avoid potential pitfalls but also how to anticipate and successfully navigate important developmental steps parents are likely to encounter when their child decides to become involved in organized sports. Lott has successfully raised three sons, all of whom became successful students, athletes, and citizens, and his thoughtful, considerate, and practical advice covers a wide range of topics, including your child's nutritional requirements, fostering discipline, practice, relationships with coaches and teammates, and, perhaps most importantly of all, commitment.

I am convinced you will find *Getting in the Game* a valuable and indispensable tool for supporting and nurturing your aspiring young athlete.

Wann Smith

Author of *Wishbone: Oklahoma Football 1959–1985*

ACKNOWLEDGMENTS

FIRST OF ALL, I need to thank God for including me in His plan. I would like to acknowledge all of my coaches and teammates for being a huge blessing in my life. Your input is the foundation of this book.

Let me express my appreciation to all the parents of the children I have had the pleasure to coach. Unknowingly, you planted the seed for this book.

To Noel Brown, my brother in God's eyes, thank you. I will always cherish you for taking the coaching journey with me.

Ray Alverez, Jim Haley, Gene Van Cleave, Carl Richter, Barry Switzer, and Bud Wilkinson, I give you my undying gratitude for your impactful influence on my life.

A special thanks to author Wann Smith for his contribution and friendship.

Above all, I would like to express my sincere gratitude and love for my family. To my wife, Beth, for helping me take my vision and make it a reality. Thank you.

To Alexander David for your enthusiasm and positivity. Thank you.

To Kristopher Keven for following two brothers and a dad who were athletes because that had to be both a curse and a blessing. You handled it like a champion. Thank you.

To T. L. for being the reason I started coaching. You being the first athlete in our family, and we both had a lot to learn. You laid the foundation for Alex and Kris. One of my most rewarding moments ever was when we won our semifinal game versus the Aggies. We both ran to each other, and you jumped into my arms. Son, thank you for all of your contributions to this book. Your foresight helped keep me on the right path with the book. Your input was more valuable than I could ever express. Now I pass the next book on to you. Thank you.

This book is dedicated to my mother, Alice Faye Elliott, my father, Thomas Lott Sr., and Isaiah Elliott.

INTRODUCTION

Train a child up in the way he should go, and when

he is old, he will not depart from it.

—PROVERBS 22:6

THE GREATEST GIFT parents can give to their child is a future. I've been around sports as long as I can remember. First, I was a kid playing with my friends, then an athlete, then a parent, and then a coach. I can honestly say that each stage helped me with the next. All in all, I have been directly involved with sports for most of my life. While some aspects of youth sports are significantly different than they were forty, thirty, or even ten years ago, there are still some parts of them that have and will always remain the same.

Some statistics estimate that there are thirty-five million US youths who play organized sports each year. In the United States, it is estimated that somewhere around 66 percent of boys and 52 percent of girls play organized sports. Approximately 85 percent of coaches are parents who are coaching their own children. Yet, a 2013 Michigan State University study showed that 37 percent of kids wished that their parents weren't even at their sporting event—that's one out of three kids on the field or court! That is remarkable and disturbing at the same time.

This book will help you understand some of the challenges involved in raising an athlete, as well as enhance the many rewards. This guide is just as much intended for adults with little or no athletic knowledge as it is for those seasoned with years of athletic exprerience. You will find suggestions to help you educate, feed, strengthen, and heal your athlete. You will also learn how to incorporate principles for coping with the many demands in the sporting world. Although the challenges will be many, the rewards can be priceless and last a lifetime.

An athletic career is born of a unique intersection of opportunity, talent, physical attributes, heart, and discipline. These things have to come together at the perfect time and in the perfect way. No one knows the perfect ratio, and if that's not complicated enough, no two people will ever have the same formula. You can have all the heart and no talent or be a physical specimen that just never gets an opportunity. An athlete can also have a ton of talent and opportunity but no discipline. For every All-Pro NFL player, First-Team All-NBA player, or Gold Glove winner, there will be at least ten people out there whom you never even heard of who are just as good, if not better.

Even if you and your child do everything correctly and by the book, the odds of your child becoming a professional athlete are dauntingly slim. Think about the pruning that happens at each level. A good high school team may have one or two players go to a top NCAA program. From that NCAA program, maybe a couple of athletes get drafted. The odds of a high school football player making it to the NFL are about one in six thousand. For a high school baseball player making it to the major league, it's about one in four thousand. Further, a high school basketball player has a one in ten thousand chance of making it to the NBA (source: Minnesota Amateur Sports Commission, Athletic Footwear Association, *USA Today* survey, Michigan State University, 2013).

I don't want you to think of this as a manual on how to fast-track your child to a scholarship or the pros but rather a collection of lessons gained from experience that will be effective on and off the field. The most magnificent thing about sports is that it's packed full of life lessons that we all want our children to learn while growing up. Kids learn teamwork, dedication to a craft, and how to deal with authority, rejection, and success—the list goes on and on. Where else can you get "on-the-job" social training in such a fun environment?

You as a parent can be right there for so many teachable moments, and if you are paying close attention, you will also learn a tremendous amount about your child. You might read things that make this seem like a parenting manual. You may wonder how household chores could have any bearing on field performance. The truth is that much of what you do around the house and within your family spills over onto the field. And you know what else? Much of what happens in the context of sports can have a direct correlation on our daily lives!

Even with my background in sports—youth leagues, high school, Division I football, and professional football—when my oldest son first decided to play, I started at the same point as everyone else. I had no manual to read or blueprint to follow. With this book, I hope to mentor you through this exciting journey. I was blessed with three sons, and each one became a successful athlete in his own right. With each son, I learned from my successes and failures coaching them on and off the field, and nothing makes me happier than sharing my experience with other parents.

There are many books available that tell you how to train an athlete but not many geared toward how to *raise* an athlete. I didn't always know it, but I've spent most of my life researching and writing this book. I have committed over half of my life to studying and testing theories, learning by trial and error, and, most importantly, evolving. Whether your four-year-old is just starting soccer or your teenager wants to start playing a sport, I'm confident that parents of athletes at all levels will be able to take something from the lessons I've learned and ultimately become valuable assets to their children.

1

STARTING OUT

Start where you are, do what you can, use what you have.

—ARTHUR ASHE

AN ATHLETE'S DEVELOPMENT begins before he or she learns to sit up. I started with my sons, Thomas, Alexander, and Kristopher, by pushing a ball back and forth, but I also watched very closely as they learned to control their heads, track moving objects, and roll over. Learning how to balance and move freely is the first step to motor-skill development. The mechanics that determine the running motion—body movement, arm and leg position, and shifting of body weight—can reveal an incredible amount of information.

Some athletes are born with an innately fluid running motion that provides them an enormous advantage, but without deliberate and proper training, they may never achieve maximum running potential. One would think running is as natural as walking, but it takes training to reach the maximum level of performance. Believe it or not, the majority of professional athletes probably never reach their maximum running potential. This is why they are constantly training.

When my eldest son, T. L., was still quite young, we owned a water bed. Even though he had just learned to walk, we were amazed to see how he was able to stand upright on the mattress, bobbing and weaving against the undulating movement of the water. I believe that his ability to maintain his equilibrium against the movement of the water bed contributed as much or more than anything else to developing his strong sense of balance, and that balance became a key asset throughout his athletic career.

I am by no means suggesting that you need a water bed, but there are plenty of other common techniques that can be used to help develop your athlete. In today's early-development marketplace, there are countless toys that can help in the development of hand-eye coordination while stimulating the brain, muscles, and nervous system. Your athlete's development can start earlier than you think.

On occasion, a child will clearly let you know when it's time to start a sport—or at least think about starting—but the decision to begin also has much to do with the individual child and the individual sport chosen. For example, my oldest son played in the grade above him in YMCA football until his teammates began playing for their junior high school. I allowed him to play when he was in second grade, while the majority of the league was in third grade because I knew he was physically and mentally mature enough. In fact, he was so much more mature that even as one of the youngest player on the team and probably in the league, I made him my quarterback because he could understand and communicate to his teammates what I was trying to accomplish as a coach. My other two sons started flag football with their peers in second grade and moved on to tackle football in third grade.

You, the parent, should know what level your child is on, but in the child's best interest, you must be honest in your evaluation. Each child and situation is different. Some kids are physically and mentally able to start sports at the age of four or five, but some sports are so physically and skillfully demanding that starting before the age of eight can be more harmful than helpful. In the early stages, it is more important to play, play, play! Don't worry—training will come later. Kick and throw balls, swing bats, jump, run, catch, and climb. At this stage, it is important to keep things fun!

While having fun is the most important part in the beginning stage of becoming an athlete, learning to compete is also a key factor. Friendly competition can be taught through not only sports but also card games, board games, and even video games (in moderation, of course). Competition is an important concept to grasp. Some children will be more competitive than others, but it is important to encourage a good balance. Too much or too little competitive spirit may not be a good thing in the early stages of development. However, it is of utmost importance to teach your child to play within the rules and respect the game. Although winning is the ultimate goal, no one wins all of the time. Teach them to not only win with class but also lose with class.

Whenever my sons and I competed in *anything* against each other, we always had a customary handshake afterward. I demanded this even before they could fully understand what I was asking of them, and thirty years later, it still concludes any game we play. It is important to show good sportsmanship and thank your opponents for the privilege of playing with them.

When one of my sons was four, he and I were shooting baskets to ten on his mini–basketball goal, as we had many times before. Being only four, he had never beaten me, and this occasion was no different. On that day he wasn't interested in any postgame displays of sportsmanship and tried to walk away without shaking my hand. This was obviously unacceptable on many levels but, more importantly, a crucial teaching moment. I extended my hand and said, "Good game," but he refused to shake it. He started to cry and put his hands behind his back. I very sternly expressed my disapproval and said, "Son, you will shake my hand and stop crying before we leave this room." After a slight hesitation, he begrudgingly shook my hand.

I sat him down at that moment and explained that playing sports is a privilege, not a right (a recurring theme you will see throughout this book). I reminded him that no one *has* to let him play sports, and it is something he had to *earn* the right to do. Finally, I told him, "You're four years old. Do you really think you can beat me in basketball? You will get older, and as you commit yourself to learning and working hard as an athlete, you'll start to beat me at many things. But right now, you are a long way from that. I have worked hard most of my life to be the athlete that I am now. If you don't like this feeling of losing, work at getting better. But no matter what happens from this day forward, you must win with class and lose with class."

COACHING POINTS: STARTING OUT

- Athletic development begins early. Toys and household objects that utilize gross motor skills and hand-eye coordination can help stimulate athletic ability.
- Each situation is different. Let your child show you when he or she is ready for sports, but also be honest in your evaluations.
- Have fun and teach healthy competition. Stress the importance of rules and respect.

2

HOW TO START

Definiteness of purpose is the starting point of all
achievement.

—W. CLEMENT STONE

BEFORE YOU BEGIN anything new in life, the first questions
you should ask yourself are these: "What am I trying to accomplish? What are my goals?" As the parent of a future athlete,
you should be asking yourself, "What do *we* want to accomplish
together?" Understand that your child may not have any idea of
what he or she wants to accomplish. Generally, a child has only

one immediate goal, and that's to play. This is where you as a parent must intercede. You should ask yourself, "Is my child ready for practice, coaching, winning, losing, and competing? Am I ready for these things?"

Organized sports can start as young as the age of four—and, on some occasions, even younger. While all three of my sons started football around first or second grade, they began playing organized sports when they were five years old.

In my opinion and for a variety of reasons, soccer has proven to be one of the best team sports for beginners. For starters, it's relatively economical. All you need is a ball, shirt, shorts, and grass cleats. And at this early stage of development, it is an excellent way to develop burgeoning athleticism without requiring any specific skill level. Also, aside from the occasional collision or being hit with a ball—something that could happen in most sports—the likelihood of being injured is low.

The object of the game is simple: run and kick a ball into a goal. Some players will aggressively swarm to the ball, while others will timidly stay as far from it as possible. As with any group activity in life, there will be varying degrees of ability; some players will come to the forefront, while others will contently fade into the background. And that's OK! Your child will gain beneficial experience from being part of a team by working with others and competing. That is the most important part of this stage, although, to your child, wearing the uniform will probably be the biggest thrill!

The good news is that you can literally start anywhere! Backyards, front yards, driveways, and parks are simple and accessible places to start playing a sport. There are plenty of organizations to get involved in, such as a YMCA, YWCA, or Boys and Girls Club, just to name a few. More and more churches are starting sports leagues as well. It's easy to research the different opportunities and leagues your budding athlete may have at his or her disposal. However, make sure you do your due diligence; not all leagues are created equal, so you'll want to research thoroughly and ask lots of questions. Different leagues will have different rules, game days, and practice limitations. It's important to know what you're getting into before you and your child take this step.

It is also important to stress to your child that part of being on a team is honoring your commitment. If the decision to join a team for a season is made, it must be seen through at all costs. I cannot stress the importance of teaching your athlete that once something is started, it must be seen through to completion. I'll discuss this in more detail in chapter 7. As a coach, I have seen athletes who were allowed to walk away from a sports commitment by his or her parent because things got hard or the sport didn't come as naturally as it did to others. This is a dangerous precedent to establish. I can assure you that once you quit on a commitment, it can quickly become a bad habit.

COACHING POINTS: HOW TO START

- Determine the reason for starting sports and what goal is to be accomplished by doing so.
- Soccer is an excellent beginning sport because it's inexpensive to play and relatively safe.
- Stick with your commitment. If the decision to join a team has been made, then the athlete must honor his or her commitment.

3

UNDERSTANDING THE TEAM CONCEPT

The strength of the team is each
individual member.
The strength of each individual member
is the team.
—PHIL JACKSON

S PORTS ARE ALL about great moments. Some of the most memorable events in my life have involved sports, some of which also included my sons. My most satisfying moments have come from the realization of great teamwork. Any former athlete will reflect fondly on events of past games, but most of their best memories will involve bus rides, hotel stays, and meals with teammates.

Sooner or later everyone will be a part of a team. Whether as part of a family, in sports, or in the workforce, understanding the team concept and being able to function within the framework of a team is particularly important in our society. No one is successful without the help of other people somewhere along the way.

Your athlete's first experience working with others will naturally come from within your family. Having brothers and sisters is an ongoing social interaction and exercise in sharing. Even if your athlete is an only child, he or she will take part in activities with other children. While it is important that we teach our children how to conduct themselves with others, you can get a good glimpse of how your child will function in a team environment from closely observing his or her behavior in a group setting.

There is no doubt that our personalities are still forming throughout our childhood—partly from our experiences and partly from the biological maturity of our brains—but some components of our personalities are in place from the moment we are born. Think back to when your child was nine months old. Almost certainly, there were some behaviors you thought were simply baby traits at the time, but they ended up being early manifestations of his or her personality.

An athlete's personality will have a bearing on how he or she functions as a part of a team—on and off the field.

From the time your child begins to walk, he or she will be busy. Children's curiosity will compel them to get into anything and everything within their reach. So why not put that energy to productive use by encouraging them to start helping "the team"? Have them pick things up off the floor and put them where they belong or throw things away for you. I laugh at my son because he asks his little girl to take her clothes to the washer—one by one! And you know what? *She loves every second of it!* What little toddler wouldn't want to (1) help or hang out with Mom or Dad and (2) walk, walk, walk! Take advantage while they are actually interested in helping you.

Once they get the hang of helping, they will be more than willing to show you what they can do. Praise them, teach them early, and as they grow, they will be proud of their accomplishments. Within a family, every member has an obligation to do whatever he or she can to help the family prosper, and it is important to communicate that early. My high school head football coach, Gene VanCleave, constantly stressed the importance of each team member having a job and focusing solely on executing *that* job. Give them little tasks to complete, and they will be glad to own them.

As they get older, they will be able to fully understand the team concept.

In an organized team environment, coaches, teammates, and supporters will all become your extended family. You will often hear teammates refer to themselves as brothers or sisters. High school and college coaches will generally spend as much or more time with their athletes as they do with their own children, so in a very real sense, their players become family. In order for the team to succeed, everyone—coaches and players—must do their part.

Once you and your child decide to join the sporting world, you become obligated to do everything you can to help the team. Parents must understand that this not only affects their developing athlete but that it's a family commitment. There will be many changes in your home structure that will affect everyone, athletes and nonathletes alike. Practice, game, and transportation times have to be worked in, and study time and family time as well as other obligations must be honored. As a result, sacrifices will have to be made by everyone in the process. The more athletes you have in your household, the more drastic the change will be! If you have never been very organized, this is an excellent time to begin. Get a dry-erase calendar to write down game, practice, and meeting times and become attached to it. Display it in plain sight because it's going to be a team effort, and it's important to have the schedule in a common area.

One of the most important aspects of an athlete's development is practice. Unless it's an emergency, missing practice or games is not an option. There will never be enough time at a team practice to get each individual the help that he or she needs, so here is when you, as the parent, come in. You simply cannot underestimate the importance of your involvement. Sometimes a little backyard reinforcement of going over something new learned at practice goes a long way.

Feedback is essential, so communicate with the coach and ask what your athlete needs to work on. Make sure you and the coach are on the same page and that you aren't contradicting anything that he or she is teaching. If you practice with your athlete for just thirty minutes four days a week, that's an extra two hours of practice that most of the other players on the team aren't getting!

Another essential part of being on a team is academics. Mental and physical development go hand in hand—you can't have one without the other and compete on a high level. When I was coaching, I would tell my athletes that you can't "dummy up" all day in the classroom and then make split-second decisions while playing your sport. Your brain is just like any other muscle, and it must be trained and kept sharp. Most people do not realize that there is quite a bit of studying that goes into playing sports. An athlete *should* know his responsibilities and eventually everyone else's on each and every play. It is possible to get by on talent alone, but to really excel, you must be a student of the game.

Demand accountability in the classroom as well. Make sure you are checking your child's homework and do not accept a haphazard effort in school. One of my sons sat out an entire season because of an unacceptable effort in school.

That being said, when the athlete is on the field of play, he or she should be on the field of play. I wouldn't expect any of my athletes to be thinking about homework or tests when they are at practice or during a game. I would also expect them to be fully engaged and focused on the task at hand when they are in class. I think one of the biggest perpetuated myths in our fast-paced society is the supposed skill of multitasking. Humans aren't designed to do more than one thing at a time. So-called multitaskers don't juggle multiple things at the same time but instead focus on one job, ensure it's done well, and then efficiently move on to the next task. This is precisely how the most successful student-athletes operate. Between your family, school, and sports obligations, your child will have many opportunities to practice working and collaborating with others.

COACHING POINTS: UNDERSTANDING THE TEAM CONCEPT

- Teamwork is a part of life. From the moment you enter this world, you are part of a team.
- Teach your children that they are part of a "team" and, as a parent, always find ways for them to contribute to the greater good of the family.
- Your sports team is an extended family. Your family time may be disrupted, so it is important to keep a tight schedule and work in new sports obligations with existing family and school obligations.
- A team is like a chain. It is only as strong as its weakest link.

4

From a Coach's Point of View

I think what coaching is all about, is taking players
and analyzing their ability, put them in a position
where they can excel within the framework of the
team winning.

—Don Shula

COACHING IS A difficult undertaking. Much like a parent, a
coach will often receive unjustified credit for positive results and undue blame for negative results. A coach is essentially
the CEO and the face of the team. While charged with being the
head decision-maker and executor (which also means ultimate

accountability), his or her number-one job is to create an environment in which each *individual* member of the team can thrive. In return, happy team members are the foundation of a successful organization.

A good coach must have the ability to wear many different hats. We might initially think of a coach as just a teacher, but he or she must also have the ability to simultaneously fill the role of counselor, friend, confidant, disciplinarian, and even occasionally bus driver.

When introducing your young athlete to the world of sports, it is of paramount importance to find the right coach. While you almost never get to handpick a coach, it's important to pay close attention to your options. As with teachers, there are many different coaching methods and styles. Some will work well with certain personalities and not so well with others. A clash of personality styles between a player and a coach can make for a long, miserable season and leave a child with a negative outlook on sports down the road. However, as in life, we will undoubtedly encounter and must learn to work with difficult bosses, professors, or leaders. In most cases, this type of conflict shouldn't prevent the development of a successful working relationship! Do not let anything, or anyone, distract you from your goal.

Always remember that you as the parent, fan, and supporter of your child have a different primary objective than that of a coach. Your main focus is on your athlete and what he or she is doing, feeling, and thinking. A good coach's job is to be concerned about *every* athlete on the team and, most importantly, the greater good of the group.

Doc Rivers, head coach of the Los Angeles Clippers, correctly pointed out, "You've got to coach worrying about your entire team: whether that gets you a championship or whether that gets you fired." A coach must be mindful of not putting any one individual above the team—including him- or herself. Coaches often have to make hard decisions to benefit the group as a whole (with or without input from the team), and those may not always agree with an individual athlete's own agenda.

While a parent must be careful to respect boundaries, it's important to be involved and to attend practice occasionally so you can gain insight into what goes into a week of game preparation. It's not always possible to speak with the coach right before or immediately after practice, but you also can't rely entirely on input from your athlete, especially a young one.

I once coached a young player who had shown in practice that he was not mentally ready to go into a game. He was incredibly fearful and timid, so I planned to select his playing time strategically in very specific game situations. Football is a sport where tiptoeing around with the fear of getting injured is actually a great way to get hurt. As a coach, I did what I could to allow him to gain some experience on the field. With a limited roster, I felt wide receiver would be a good position because it kept him relatively removed from most of the action and collisions.

When I finally decided to send him into the game, he hesitated and said, "Coach, I have a problem." When I asked him what his problem was, he answered, "I'm scared!" as he had said many times in practice. I put my hand on his shoulder and told him that he didn't have to go in if he didn't want to. He could stand next to me, and he did for the entire game. After the game, his parents questioned me about why he didn't play. They told me that their son had been coming home every day after practice and telling them how well he was doing and how much better he was than the other players on the team. Although this particular set of parents had always dropped off and picked up their son from practice, they had never actually attended a practice or communicated with me, so they had no idea of how he was doing.

I decided to let the athlete tell his parents the real story, so I called him over and asked him to be honest with himself, his parents, and me as to why he didn't play in the game. He then told us that he was scared to play. Needless to say, this removed a critical roadblock in his progress, and we all got on the same page that afternoon.

If your child is not getting as much playing time as he or she wants or as much as you think he or she should be receiving, attend a practice unannounced and see for yourself how your child is progressing. All coaches want to win, and with that in mind, they *should* be playing the best players. If your child is not getting to play in the game, the answer could lie on the practice field.

I highly recommend setting an appointment for a private meeting with the coach to discuss what you can do to help your athlete. The goal of this meeting should never be for you to advocate more playing time for your athlete but rather to find out what you can do to help your athlete improve his or her own personal progress and that of the team. No coach wants to be told whom he or she should play, and in most situations, this tactic will create resentment, or, even worse, it could backfire. A coach should be open to any suggestions that might help the team, so approaching him or her from the angle of what your athlete might be able to contribute should result in a tangible answer and actionable strategy for you to employ at home. It's also important to only speak in terms of your athlete and not bring up other teammates. Remember: this conversation should be about helping your athlete and therefore helping the team.

Holidays and vacations should be taken into consideration during any particular sports season. Each year many families go on vacations that can leave teams shorthanded. Most programs and leagues take these dates into consideration, but you should always plan around your team practices and games. It is difficult to hold practice without a complete team in attendance, so when you sign up for any sport, you should be at every practice and at every game. This is your commitment. Keep in mind that coaches have to be at every practice and at every game as well. They, too, would love to be home with their family but must be totally committed. Every athlete should be also.

Always keep in mind that coaching is a complex job, and many factors go into final preparation on game day. I can sincerely say that every coach I've ever played for has in some way directly influenced not only my sports career but also my life. I continue to use the lessons I learned from these people every day. As in every walk of life, there are good leaders and bad leaders. A good coach will value teaching his players life lessons more than winning at any cost.

Important Teaching Points a Coach Should Be Stressing	A Coach's Duties and Responsibilities
Build confidence	Protect athletes
Develop good work ethic	Protect the program
Work within a team	Be truthful
Develop accountability and communication skills	Earn trust and develop relationships
Promote loyalty and dependability	Be a good listener
Have respect	Keep lines of communication open between players and parents
Be prepared to sacrifice	Be a problem solver

COACHING POINTS: FROM A COACH'S POINT OF VIEW

- Coaching is not an easy task. As with a CEO role, there is an incredible amount of planning and managing of many personalities that goes into a successfully run organization.

- Make sure to actively attend practice so you can see how your child is participating and what goes into each week of preparation.

- A coach has a different agenda from the parent. You are concerned with the welfare of one individual; whereas, the coach is concerned with the welfare of many individuals but ultimately the group as a whole.

- If you feel something isn't going right, set up a meeting with the coach and approach it from the angle of how you and your athlete can best help the team.

5

COMPETE RIGHT AWAY

The important thing in life is not to triumph, but

to compete.

—PIERRE DE COUBERTIN

AN IMPORTANT ASPECT of youth sports is that it provides a safe and controlled environment that promotes learning while fostering a healthy, competitive spirit. Learning to compete is critical to one's success because, at some point, each of us will need to "beat" someone at something to achieve a goal. It is difficult to clearly define the complicated set of biological and environmental factors that combine to make certain individuals more competitive and aggressive than others.

You can help your child develop a competitive mind-set and a desire to win (or be the best at something) by celebrating his or her accomplishments. Young children crave approval from their parents, so give them praise when they do well. Whether it's a round of applause for taking a few steps, cheers for finishing dinner, or high fives after completing a task, it's never too early for them to experience that great feeling of achievement.

It's also important to use a "failure" as a teaching moment. To quote the Dalai Lama, "When you lose, don't lose the lesson." Teach your child/young athlete that an unsuccessful attempt at anything is always a chance to correct and improve. As the child gets older, there are definitely distinct benefits in celebrating accomplishments, but being constructively critical also has its place. I believe positive reinforcement is the best tool for building a confident young child, but there is a fine line that can be crossed when undue or excessive praise for every little thing breeds a sense of entitlement.

Bear in mind that when praise is withheld or when criticism is too heavily administered, a permanent sense of defeat and hopelessness can develop. Make sure you don't dish out too much of either. Remember that a healthy balance between the two approaches is essential.

Parents should always be preparing their athlete for the next level. By next level, I don't necessarily mean professional sports, but rather whatever that next step might be. We do this each year in our educational system. Kindergartners are being groomed for first grade; high school students are preparing for college; and sports are no different. If your child is in the second-grade league, watch a third-grade game. Observe the speed of the game and how it is played overall. You will undoubtedly notice some skills to work on for the next season. However, do not place too much emphasis on that next stage. It will come soon enough. Your main focus should remain on your child's current stage of development.

If you asked one hundred of the most successful people in the United States what personal traits they attribute to their success, I guarantee you that *discipline* would be in everyone's top five. You can't be successful in anything without having discipline, and it's never too early to start teaching this to your child.

Mandatory daily routines, such as making the bed, keeping clothes neatly put away, and setting the table, are simple ways to begin teaching discipline. You can also do your children an enormous favor by not accepting subpar effort or results (remember: don't overly praise). If the bed has lumps in it, have them go back until the job is done correctly. Resist the urge to jump in and do it for them. By doing this, you will avoid dealing with their objections, and you will make them happy for the moment, but you will also be sending the wrong message.

In Jay Bilas's book *Toughness,* a colleague of his describes discipline as "doing what you *should* do over what you *want* to do" and maturity as "when what you *want* to do is what you're *supposed* to do." The ultimate goal for every parent should be for his or her external voice of instruction to eventually be replaced by the child's own internal voice—when making the bed shifts from doing something that Mom and Dad said to do to having a personal desire for his or her space to be neat and well kept. This won't happen overnight. Sports or no sports, teaching self-discipline and good habits takes persistence and patience!

While having a competitive spirit is an important factor in being successful, simply *wanting* to be better than your competition in and of itself isn't enough. This only leads to frustration and demotivation. Helping your child develop the self-discipline to prepare for the next level is a key ingredient. Those with high levels of self-discipline actually learn to compete with *themselves*, so they become intrinsically motivated and seek their "rewards" from within.

Coaching Points: Compete Right Away

- Competitive desire is part nature and part nurture, but it is essential to success. Playing sports can be a safe and controlled way to introduce the concept of healthy competition.

- As you compete, you should be preparing for the next level. Be aware of what is necessary to ascend to the next tier.

- To be a worthy competitor, self-discipline is absolutely critical. You can foster this skill at home with persistence and patience. Ultimately, the goal is for your young athletes to do things the right way because *they* want to.

6

Participation versus Winning

Success is not final, failure is not fatal. It is courage
to continue that counts.

—Winston Churchill

ALTHOUGH THERE HAVE been some positive changes in youth sports today, some changes have not been so positive. We seem to have entered an era where we award all young participants in any endeavor equally and deliberately to avoid the concept of "winning" or "losing." This type of approach is the root cause of an entitled generation. While it is quite true that participating in a sport is a critical first step, it is far from the end game.

I am a strong opponent of participation awards. Awarding participation doesn't promote hard work, sacrifice, or commitment, nor does it reward actual competitive accomplishment. Instead, a child enters the season knowing that he or she will not only get a trophy but also will receive the same exact trophy as every other participant in the league regardless of performance, behavior, attitude, or attendance. A child's team wins all their games? There is a trophy at the end of the season. A child cries every time he or she strikes out? Another trophy at the end of the season. A basketball team makes two baskets all season? Trophy at the end of the season. So what exactly is the lesson here?

Proponents will argue that a focus on winning detracts from the fundamentals or that winning inevitably becomes the sole focus, and we forget about our children's development. Perhaps if we turned off the scoreboard during a youth soccer game, the sport itself would become the sole focus while completely eliminating the concepts of competition, winners, and losers.

This may sound great in theory, but that's not how things work in this world and certainly not in this country. The United States was built upon people winning and people losing. How did you get your job? You beat someone out because you were better. How are you going to rise up in the ranks and get that promotion? You're going to have to be better at something than your peers. When you suffer a defeat or failure, how are you going to rebound?

Competition is all around us, and if you're going to enjoy any level of success, you'll have to know how to compete and win. This is an important lesson that kids have to learn as early as possible. Stripping this concept from sports robs our children of an important opportunity to learn to deal with both failure *and* success. Believe me, they will need as much practice as they can get enduring one and enjoying the other. Remember, both extremes can be character builders.

With this "no winners or losers" approach, our athletes (and kids in general) develop a mentality that they should be rewarded for simply showing up. Can you blame them? They've been rewarded and applauded for every trivial accomplishment since they began "competing." They develop an expectation that if they just work hard at their sport, they should be rewarded with something.

Let me take this opportunity to bust a long-standing myth about work. Working on the practice field or the playing field doesn't mean you deserve anything. It only puts you in the position for good things to happen. During my youth, I was told "practice makes perfect." When I started coaching, I learned that was not a true statement. *Perfect practice makes perfect.* It allows you to free your mind so you're reacting instead of thinking. That's it. Work does not guarantee that your number will get called or even that your performance will be up to par, but not working at all will guarantee failure.

When my son Alex was just starting to play youth basketball, his team won their first six games. On the seventh game, they lost for the first time. I remember him crying after the game, so I pulled him aside and asked him about it. He said he was crying because they had lost. Our conversation then went like this:

"Did you do everything you could to help your team win?"

"Yes."

"How many days this week other than practice did you dribble the basketball?"

"None."

"How many times this week did you shoot the basketball other than at practice?"

"None."

"How many times outside of practice did you shoot free throws?"

"Well, none."

"Then you have not done everything you could do to help your team win, so you have not earned the right to cry or complain. If it was not important enough for you to put in the extra work this week, why is it so important now? If you don't like this feeling, then do something before the game—because if you wait until the game, it will be too late. Practice with the team will never be enough."

From that moment on, Alex always put in the extra time.

Winning should be the ultimate goal, and it's important not to reinforce failure or reward mediocrity. It drives me crazy to hear people yell, "It's OK!" from the stands after a player has made a mistake. You don't want your athlete to dwell on a mistake, but at the same time, it's not really just OK either. The only thing this does is confuse a young athlete. He or she must be able to distinguish between what is really OK and what isn't.

Knute Rockne once said, "Show me a good and gracious loser, and I'll show you a failure." I don't necessarily think that Knute was talking about skipping the postgame handshakes, but it speaks to a larger point that if you fail at something, you shouldn't be OK with it. You should want your athlete to develop a sour taste in his or her mouth when he or she fails that can only be cured by success.

Human beings inherently want to improve, but in many cases the only way we know that improvement is necessary is from external feedback. So if all the messages being fed are that "it's OK" and "you're doing great," why would the athlete feel the need to improve anything? What's going on around him to trigger that urge? Think about some of the fiercest competitors in memory: Muhammad Ali, Michael Jordan, Serena Williams, Mia Hamm, and Peyton Manning. They have all won and love to keep winning. However, what really drives them is to never experience that sour taste of failure.

Winning a championship remains one of the most difficult of human accomplishments, and very few people achieve it. If your athlete happens to be one of the chosen few who has experienced ultimate victory, cherish that moment because he or she will always be a champion, and no one can ever take that away from him or her. It should be celebrated because it takes commitment, dedication, sacrifice, hard work, and little bit of luck. It's perfectly appropriate to recognize success, but it's also critical that your athlete learn to handle success.

We had a shelf for all the trophies in our house, but first-place trophies and medals always went in the first row for all to see. We would even have a little award ceremony each time one of my sons won a championship or earned a first-place award. We'd toast with sparkling grape juice, and I'd say a few words about the recipient's season and accomplishment. The recipient was also obliged to say a few words to the group. It was important to me that my sons learned how to win with class but also to speak in front of supporters with elegance.

My boys and I have each lost a championship game, and while I do not believe in so-called moral victories, I know the disappointment we've each experienced prepared us to handle future hardships life will throw our way. Some of my biggest heartbreaks have happened because of sports. The sting of losing the last game of an undefeated season at John Jay High School still vividly resonates with me half a century later. While I'd love to go back and change things, I can at least begrudgingly admit that I learned a few life lessons that day. Remembering times like those when things were tough has served as a coping mechanism that I still use today. After all the years of blood, sweat, and tears that I left on the football field, I know there is nothing life can throw me that I can't handle.

In today's entitled society, participation awards belittle the accomplishments and hard work required to go through a season.

Sadly, by simply signing up and paying a registration fee, your child is often guaranteed an award. That's not a whole lot different than just saving the time and gas money and buying a trophy. If learning fundamentals both in sports and in life is your priority, then we must convey the lessons that keeping score provides. We must draw a distinct line between winning and losing, because whether we do or not, life does. That's one of the most fundamental lessons of all.

COACHING POINTS: PARTICIPATION VERSUS WINNING

- Participation should be appreciated but not rewarded. We don't deserve anything for simply showing up.

- We all have to "win" at something in our lives—this country was built on winners and losers. It's important that we don't rob our children of learning this concept early.

- There is a difference between moving on from a mistake and ignoring it. We shouldn't say something is OK if there is legitimate improvement to be made.

- Talent is God-given, so be humble. Fame is human-given, so be thankful. Conceit is self-given, so be careful.

7

DON'T PUSH—GUIDE

It is one thing to show your child the way, and a

harder thing to then stand out of it.

—ROBERT BRAULT

TOO MANY PARENTS try to live their lives through their children. We've all known "those" parents who just know that they have the next superstar millionaire on their hands. They drive and drive their child until sometimes it's hard to tell where they end and the child begins!

Think about this: how many times have you seen this type of parent end up (1) with their goal reached, and, more importantly,

(2) a healthy relationship gained with their child? Probably not very often. I can't stress this enough: *you shouldn't push your child into anything, but definitely don't push your child into sports.* Your job as a parent is to guide your children and help them find their way in life. This couldn't be truer than in the context of sports.

I never asked any of my three sons if they wanted to play a sport; I just exposed them to sports and let them come to me if they were interested. Because of my football background, people assumed that my kids would be funneled into that particular sport as soon as they could walk. I'm here to tell you that nothing could be further from the truth. My oldest son decided to give football a try as soon as he was old enough. He didn't tell me this until many years later, but whenever we would visit my mother, she would always find a way to pull him aside and ask him if he really wanted to play football. She would assure him he didn't have to if he didn't want to. Each time she asked, he said he told her that he played because he wanted to, and I believe that was the honest truth.

When one of my sons showed an interest in a particular sport, I made sure that I showed interest also and exposed him to the basic fundamental aspects of that activity. Watching games together, talking about the sport, and practicing or playing with your child are good introductions to a sport before even considering joining a league. At the end of the day, you know your child best, so you'll be able to tell the difference between a genuine and a fleeting interest. If you can't tell, continue letting him or her explore and keep evaluating. Remember: sports aren't for everyone. If you have more than one child, not all of them may be athletically inclined. While all three of my boys became athletes, they were three very different kinds of athletes, each with his own unique set of abilities.

It is vital that your child makes his or her own choice to play and not be pushed or coerced into playing any sport. A young child has no idea what he or she wants in general, let alone if he or she wants to be an athlete. Your job is to help provide information and support if you see an interest. If you have pushed your son or daughter into a sport, when things get tough—whether it be during the season or just an overall dissatisfaction with the sport—there will be some level of resentment toward you as a parent.

Have you ever been led or made to do something you didn't want to do? When things start to get difficult, it's really easy to point that finger at someone else. You can avoid that scenario altogether if you aren't doing the driving. It's critical that you provide direction but not direct. Think of yourself as being in the passenger seat while teaching your son or daughter how to drive. You can help; you can assist; you can provide direction; but, no matter how badly you might want to, you can't drive!

Once the decision has been made to join a league, make sure it is a year-to-year (or season to season) commitment—no more and no less. If he or she decides not to continue the following season, you should be equally as supportive. However, starting and then quitting during the season should not be an option. The only way to get a true picture is to experience a full season. Your athlete must go through all phases of a season to get a true feel for the commitment, hard work, and the ultimate rewards. The ups and downs, turnarounds, successes, and failures are part of what makes a season—and life for that matter! Every championship season has its bumps in the road, and every losing season has some positive moments.

I once coached a team that started out 0–3, which left us one game from play-off elimination. We proceeded to win every subsequent game until losing by one point in the championship game. I've also seen a team go winless and then, after winning their final game of the season, celebrate like they had won the championship.

I can't express enough how important it is for your child to experience this—for reasons much more important than sports. It's all right to express some disappointment and not plan on returning the following season, but it's more important to remind your athlete the commitment he or she made and must honor. This is an important life lesson. It is imperative to know that it is not OK to walk away and quit anything midstream. Allowing your son or daughter to quit is setting a bad precedent for how to deal with future hardships because it is inevitable they'll experience more. It may seem trivial at the time, but time and time again, I have seen it grow into bigger issues later in life when a child is in a situation where he or she must follow through with a problem. You never want to send the message that quitting on your teammates, coaches, or anyone counting on you is acceptable. Life is a team effort.

You may be thinking, "I don't want to make my children do anything they don't want to do." Completing a season is not the same thing as forcing your child to do something they don't want to do. It's essential that they learn that if a commitment is made (don't forget—it was his or her idea), that commitment must be honored. This applies to you as the parent also. While it may be tempting to have your schedule freed from practice and games, you too made a commitment and must set an example for your athlete by honoring it. Don't worry, you'll get your Saturdays back before you know it!

Even when your child has developed a love for a sport, it can be difficult for a parent to tell the difference between pushing and guiding. I have been guilty of pushing. When my son Kris was nine years old, I wanted him to play quarterback on the team that I was coaching because his knowledge of the game matched his athletic ability. Although I knew wide receiver was his first love followed by running back, there were some games that I would bribe him to play quarterback for my own selfish reason: I wanted to win. After these games, I would always need to apologize to Kris for having pushed him. I knew better than anyone what the pressure of playing this stressful position felt like. Kris disliked the anxiety, just as I had.

So make sure that you are walking alongside your athlete as a guide. You shouldn't be pushing them from behind, nor should you be out in front dragging them along. Support their interests by showing an interest yourself and allow them to make the ultimate decision to pursue or not to pursue a sport. If the decision is made to join a league, honor that commitment for at least the duration of the season. It is perfectly fine to walk away after the season is over if he or she isn't having fun, but not a moment before. There's only one reason for your child to be an athlete: because he or she wants to.

COACHING POINTS: DON'T PUSH—GUIDE

- Don't push your child into sports. Keep an eye on their interest and create opportunities to learn more before making the commitment to a league or team.
- Commitment to a league/team should be on a year-to-year basis.
- Barring an injury, your athlete should not be permitted to quit during the season. This is sending the message that it is OK to quit when things get tough.
- Be mindful not to put your interests ahead of your child's interests.

8

HEALTH AND NUTRITION

Tell me what you eat, and I'll tell you who you are.

—JEAN ANTHELME BRILLAT-SAVARIN

EACH INDIVIDUAL IS unique in his or her own way. Modern technology has answered many questions as to how the human body works, but when it comes to fitness and nutrition, there are still and always will be many debates about what to put in your body to get maximum performance.

Hundreds of diets, vitamins, and supplements have come into play over the last twenty years. It's easy to become overwhelmed while shopping at a nutrition store or perusing a health-and-fitness magazine or website. Although I do not profess to be a nutritionist or doctor, I would like to share a few observations from my own experiences being an athlete and coach and raising three athletes. My goal here is to give you a few points to stimulate your awareness about what you feed your athlete. It's always important to consult with your doctor or pediatrician about anything you put in your athlete's body.

IT ALL STARTS WITH A BALANCED DIET

Optimal nutrition is an integral part of peak performance and a key factor in the final product you see on the field. What exactly is optimal nutrition, and how can you achieve it?

The Mayo Clinic recommends an individual get 45 to 65 percent of their daily calories from carbohydrates, 10 to 35 percent of daily calories from protein, and 20 to 35 percent from fat. Each individual processes fuel differently, so adjust these ratios according to your athlete.

Each of my three sons had different ways of metabolizing their fuel, so I kept that in mind in the way I fed them. Just remember that drastically increasing or decreasing carbohydrates, proteins, or fats can have some adverse effects.

It is important to plan meals for the week. Use Saturday or Sunday to decide what will be eaten for the rest of the week. This will not only allow you to have the ability to sit down and plan smart meals but will also free you from having to come up with what to eat on the fly during a busy week of school and practice. Consider cooking multiple meals and freezing them, which makes an even quicker go-to weeknight meal.

Resist the urge to skip or skimp on breakfast. It truly is the most important meal of the day and sets the body's metabolic tone for the next twenty-four–hour period. The body is very much like a car, and the better the quality of fuel that goes into your body, the better it will perform. Lunch can be a little heavier meal because this will be the fuel used in an after-school practice, although too heavy of a lunch can make for a sleepy afternoon! After school, a light, healthy snack is good, especially on practice days. After practice, dinner and a good night's sleep will help replenish damaged cells. Getting rest is absolutely critical for an athlete's development, so make sure that a decent bedtime is established.

CARBOHYDRATES

Carbohydrates provide your body with energy. Athletes specifically need more carbohydrates in their diet than the average nonathlete. Carbs provide the primary source of fuel for exercising muscles. When a person eats carbs in the form of sugars and starches, they are digested and circulated through the bloodstream as glucose, a simple sugar. If the glucose is not used immediately for energy, it will go into storage as glycogen in the liver and muscles. When these glycogen stores are filled, the excess glucose is stored as fat. As exercise continues and more energy is needed, glycogen breaks down to release the glucose as fuel for the muscles. During intense training or competition, the glycogen stores become low or depleted, and exhaustion can quickly occur.

The best way to avoid this effect is to eat the right balance of simple and complex carbohydrates. Athletes should eat more complex (slow to digest) carbohydrates than simple (quick to digest) carbohydrates. Complex carbohydrates also keep the appetite at bay much longer than simple carbohydrates. Only carbohydrates can build up glycogen stores—not protein, fat, vitamins, or minerals. Because of the importance of carbohydrates as a fuel source, low-carb diets are not a good choice for an athlete—especially on game day.

PROTEINS

The primary function of protein is to build and repair tissue. Each time we exercise, our muscles experience microtears, and protein helps to mend and restore the muscle fibers. Examples of foods high in protein are meat, beans, and eggs. It's easy to see why athletes think that more protein would mean greater muscle, but that isn't the case. Our bodies can only utilize a certain amount of protein. Since we have little capacity to store protein, any excess may be converted to fat if it is not burned. So picking up the bar with 50 grams of protein over the 25-gram variety after a workout does not mean twice the muscle gain. It instead means an almost certain excess that the body will end up having to store. The amount of protein needed by your athlete is mainly determined by his or her weight and activity level.

FATS

Fat is a substance found in certain foods that helps keep the body warm and also helps the body store energy. In addition to adequate amounts of carbs and protein, a young athlete must also consume some fat to complete a well-balanced, nutritionally adequate diet. Dietary fat is a concentrated source of calories in our diet. Fat is necessary to provide essential free fatty acids, which transport certain vitamins throughout the body. The body does not begin to use stored fat as an energy source until after about thirty to forty-five minutes of continuous exercise. Taking in large amounts of fat (as in the average American diet) can prove to be very detrimental not only to one's appearance and health but also to athletic performance.

Fat, however, is not always the enemy. There are good fats like those found in nuts, avocados, salmon, or olive oil that are better choices than trans and saturated fats found in red meat, butter, or cheese. Be leery of products claiming to be low fat, as they typically replace the fat with unhealthy additives and other undesirable replacements that are sometimes worse than the fat itself.

DRINKS

If nothing else, there is one thing in particular that an athlete should pay close attention to: staying hydrated. Replacing lost water is often neglected by athletes. It is important to remember this: *just because you aren't thirsty doesn't mean you're well hydrated.* As a matter of fact, once an athlete becomes thirsty, he or she is already facing dehydration.

Fluid loss is more rapid than most athletes realize and must be replaced as soon as possible. During two-a-day practices, it is common for the players to be weighed before and after each practice to monitor any significant weight loss. A steep drop in weight indicates a loss of important fluids and electrolytes, so it's important to watch these weight fluctuations.

For competition it's wise to start hydrating the day before an event as well as replenishing both during and after. One pint of water lost in the body equals one pound of body weight lost. Some studies have shown that loss of fluid equal to as little as 2 percent of body mass is sufficient to cause a detectable decrease in performance.

There are many sports drinks on the market today, so be careful to read the labels. Many of the so-called health drinks have little or no health benefits and way too much sugar. Sports drinks are acceptable and certainly better than juice or soda, but in my opinion there is no substitute for plain, simple water.

SUPPLEMENTS AND OTHER CHEMICALS

The fitness-nutrition market has become a lucrative enterprise. The quest for a "magic pill" is as old as time. One of the problems with supplements is that most people don't realize how easy it is to put one on the market. Manufacturers aren't required to get FDA approval before producing or selling dietary supplements. In other words, producing and selling a supplement is not a rigorous or heavily regulated endeavor and is really no more difficult than launching a website. That alone should raise a red flag.

I would be highly cautious introducing any supplements into my athlete without a doctor's recommendation. Even then, I would still do my own research and weigh the benefits and side effects. If you aren't 100 percent sure, you should have no qualms about leaving the supplement on the shelf. Barring a specific biological condition, our body will produce everything it needs when fueled by a healthy diet. Supplements should only be used if you are fully assured some areas of your individual athlete are lacking in their normal development, as opposed to intending for them to enhance performance.

The human body is a complex machine, but it's important to remember that, with proper nourishment, it's generally capable of producing everything it needs and efficiently using food. The human body was designed to only utilize a certain amount of anything that goes into it. Any excess or shortage can have adverse effects on normal development.

I can say that I never used any supplements throughout my entire athletic career and did not allow my sons to do so either. I have the strong belief that with proper training, in conjunction with a healthy diet, an athlete can reach his or her peak performance. Give them some foods they like and a lot of foods their bodies need. At the end of the day, you can never go wrong with a balanced diet. That being said, there is also no substitute for a well-informed parent, so do some research regarding what you feel comfortable putting in your athlete's body.

INJURIES

As surely as there is a winner and a loser, there will always be dings and injuries. There is, however, a difference between being *hurt* and being *injured*. Every athlete will have to play hurt at some time. In a physical game like football, an athlete ceases being "100 percent" after the first day of camp! You can't possibly imagine the weekly conditioning and therapy employed to prepare an athlete to play on game day.

Bumps and bruises shouldn't keep a player out of competition. However, when a player is injured, he or she cannot and should not play, and a coach and his or her staff should be trained to tell the difference.

Additionally, a trainer with CPR experience should be on the sidelines for each practice and game. Tools for emergency procedures (such as ice packs and first-aid kits) must be readily accessible. Parents should take the time to learn about injuries and how to treat them. Bruises, strains, and sprains are all perfectly treatable at home, and you can speed up recovery time significantly with a little know-how.

Always ice an injury during the first forty-eight hours. It may be tempting to grab the heating pad, but heat can accelerate inflammation at the onset of an injury, so refrain from going that route at first. Make sure to keep the affected body part elevated and try to keep it compressed if possible to limit swelling.

Most importantly, make sure your athlete gets plenty of rest. There's nothing worse than dealing with a nagging injury all season. Sometimes it's worth it to completely rest the affected area a little longer than you'd like in order to come back stronger. There's no need to be a hero by returning too soon, which often unnecessarily risks reinjury.

COACHING POINTS: HEALTH AND NUTRITION

- There is no substitute for a well-balanced diet. Too much of any one thing can lead to adverse effects.
- Read labels and consult your doctor if you're unsure about anything you might put in your athlete's body. Do your research!
- Know the difference between being hurt and injured. Take care of your athlete's body!

9

Don't be the Problem

Parents can really help, but they can also really hin-

der the development of their youngsters.

—Mike Krzyzewski (Coach K)

WHY IS IT that well-educated, mild-mannered, God-fearing people turn into raging maniacs at sporting events? Somehow it seems that the younger the age of the players, the crazier the fans sometimes act. Could it be that some parents and fans have an unrealistic perspective?

Many people feel that because they have paid for admission or someone they know is playing in a sporting event, they have the right to verbally and sometimes even physically abuse an official or referee. I would like to set the record straight. No one—absolutely no one—has the right to do this.

Purchasing a ticket only gives you the opportunity to watch the game. Without rules and laws, our society would be in chaos. The officials perform a critical function at sporting events. They are on the field to ensure that all rules are followed. There is no way any sporting event could occur without a neutral enforcing body active and present. Rules are in place to enhance the competition and protect the participants of the game. Of the millions of fans who attend sporting events each year, only a small percentage fully know and understand the rules of the particular game they are watching.

Officials are human too, and they will make mistakes, but over the course of a game, those mistakes will balance themselves out. No one play will ever win or lose a game, so give the referees and officials a break!

Conducting oneself properly at a sporting event ensures that everyone at the game will have a safe and enjoyable experience. Cheer for your team and never address the other team, players, coaches, or fans in a negative manner. Young athletes learn from your actions, so set a good example.

One year when I was coaching, we had a dad penalized because he did not like an official's call. He simply would not stop harassing the official. Not only did the official keep the call on the field, he also gave us another penalty. The dad became even more irate, so the official stopped the game and said if this individual did not leave the area completely, he would call the game, and our team would have to forfeit. The saddest thing about this was that the dad was a high school football coach.

Contrary to popular belief and despite players who say, "We play for the fans," this is not exactly true. Although players appreciate fans, they don't play for fans, nor should they. Games will be played whether no one shows up or if thousands are in the stands. Competition will start at a specific time, no matter who is in the stadium or arena. Fans undeniably make the game much more exciting and can be a factor in increased production in some players, but no sport needs fans to exist—fans need sports to exist.

An official (such as a referee or umpire) is there to make sure that players are following the rules of a game. They have the power to call off a game at any time or clear the stands and continue the game. Whether you agree or disagree with a call, you and your child should always respect the officials.

COACHING POINTS: DON'T BE THE PROBLEM

- Your presence at a contest entitles you to nothing. Spectators have no bearing on the outcome of the game.

- Officiating isn't easy. Referees are human and will make mistakes, but calls always have a way of balancing themselves out. Berating an official is only going to make it harder to officiate!

- Be respectful. Never address another team or official negatively. Set an example.

10

Is This All Really Worth It?

Whenever you have taken work in hand, you must
see it to the finish. That is the ultimate secret of
success.

—Dada Vasvani

S O NOW YOU are probably asking yourself, "Is this all really worth
it?" The answer to this question is an emphatic yes! There are
many options other than sports for boys and girls to pursue, but
how many of them cover so many lessons used in everyday life? In
one season an athlete will experience excitement, sadness, winning, losing, teamwork, sacrifice, stress, determination, hard work,

discipline, pain, success, and failure! The process of learning how to cope with these emotions is a necessary part of growing up and maturing.

Quite a few people who enter the sports world make the mistake of taking the commitment too lightly. As we've discussed previously, if you or your child isn't ready to commit to all that is involved in the sports world, you need not sign up. If you aren't able to be totally invested in the experience, it's not worth it to cheat your athlete, his or her teammates, and the organization with a halfhearted commitment.

Many times I've seen serious sports-minded people join with more casually minded athletes, and it's almost certainly a recipe for conflict. Can you remember a time when you were working on a project and a group member had one foot in and one foot out? It can be incredibly frustrating, and it provides fertile ground for resentment. While I am an advocate for sport and competition on all levels, it's better to leave it alone if you aren't able to make the full commitment—which, by the way, is perfectly fine!

I will always stand by my belief that sports provides some of the best on-the-job training for life that you can ask for. I challenge anyone to name another activity that will take a young man or woman through as much of what life will throw at them in an environment that is as equally controlled yet unpredictable. We have no idea how each season, practice, or play is going to turn out, but the skills necessary to adapt, persevere, and ultimately succeed can be learned throughout. We can see how children learn to deal with both failure and success with relatively small repercussions on their overall lives. Sport is indeed a microcosm of real life.

During one of my coaching seasons, our team needed to kick an extra point that would have won us the championship. My son, T. L., was both our quarterback and kicker, and he missed the kick. After the game, he was as devastated as I'd ever seen him before (or since). I asked him after the game if he felt he had done his best, and while he didn't want to go too much into the details of the game, I think deep down he knew that he had. He was still responsible for all three of our touchdowns but was guilt ridden for months over this one moment of the missed kick.

The truth of the matter was that we couldn't have even gotten to that point without him. I reminded him that no single play has ever won or lost any game. We had a kickoff return called back for clipping, and we missed two other extra points. To be quite honest, he never really discussed that night in depth with me until we started working on this book. Now thirty-four years old, he tells the story like this:

> I'll never forget missing that game-winning kick in the closing minutes of the championship game. To this day, the raw emotion that I felt from failing on such a grand stage was unlike anything I have ever felt in my life. But you know what? I know now that it wasn't really a "grand" stage at all. It was a sixth-grade youth football game—hardly anything that will ever register in the annals of history.
>
> However, as only a twelve-year-old, that was the ultimate stage for me, and I learned an incredible amount about myself and how to deal with defeat from that one moment. I had to face my coaches on the sideline and my friends and teammates at school, and it wasn't easy. Some people don't get the opportunity to learn these lessons until high school, or even college, and by then, there might be much more at stake. Having started youth sports at the age of five, I learned ~~many~~ lessons in success, failure, and teamwork

before I was even a teenager. I am eternally thankful for this on-the-job social and emotional training I received as a youth. It most certainly helped to prepare me for life's many curve balls ahead.

Through sports, the lessons our children learn and the lessons that we can learn about our children will be invaluable going forward in our lives. Not only will you be cheering on your son or daughter, but you will also have the chance to observe him or her in the ultimate social experiment!

It is certainly not easy and will require a team effort on the field as well as at home. The entire family will have to make sacrifices to make this work. This endeavor will take planning, coordination, and organization in your home. You will almost certainly have to be strict and firm about some things that you aren't comfortable with, but I can assure you it gets a little easier each time you do so.

As the parent, who is essentially the "coach" of the family team, your main job is to create an environment that will breed success. You'll need to preach discipline but also model it. Be as involved as you possibly can by attending the games and keeping the communication lines open with the coach. It's imperative to make sure you are an asset to the program.

Was it worth it for us? I can tell you from my own personal experience that it was 110 percent totally worth it, and I wouldn't have had it any other way. I would not be the successful person that I am today, nor would my sons be the confident, compassionate men they are, without growing up playing sports. I assure you that each member of our family would tell you the same.

I encourage you to embark on this exciting journey at least for a season. As a family, give it your all, and do things the right way. Continue to improve, and always remember that going through challenges and adversity doesn't build character—it reveals it. If you do all of this, I promise that you won't regret it in the long run. You'll almost certainly get more out of it than you could have imagined, with a few surprises along the way!

I wish you, your athlete, and your family the best of luck!

About the Author

Thomas Lott remains one of the University of Oklahoma's most celebrated alums. A native of San Antonio, Texas, Thomas was a decorated multisport high school athlete who was recognized as a Parade All-American at quarterback. After earning a scholarship to the University of Oklahoma, in addition to being a member of the 1975 National Championship team, he was the starting quarterback at OU for three years, 1976 to 1978, during which the Sooners won three Conference Championships. Thomas was a two-time All-Conference selection.

Drafted by the St. Louis Cardinals, Thomas spent several years on the professional level. In 2006, Thomas was inducted into the San Antonio Sports Hall of Fame, and in 2010, he was honored as an inductee into the Texas High School Football Hall of Fame.

Following his football career, Thomas successfully transitioned into coach and leader in the community. He has coached multiple sports including football, baseball, basketball, and track at all levels from youth to semi-pro. Thomas has also trained athletes for nearly thirty years, having helped several student-athletes earn FBS and Division 1 scholarships.

Thomas resides in Oklahoma City, where he continues to coach and train athletes. He is also a sports radio and Internet personality. For more information please visit **www.thomaslott.com**.

Thomas Lott III, the oldest son of Thomas Lott, grew up in Plano, TX. An all-area football and track athlete at Plano Senior High School, he earned a full football scholarship to Rice University where he became a two-year starter for the Rice Owls, and in 2003, led all Division-1 (FBS) running backs in yards per carry. Thomas currently resides in Fort Worth, TX with his wife and three children.

Made in the USA
San Bernardino, CA
28 May 2016